Notes for teachers and parents

Equipment needed:

scales
egg cup
teaspoon
fork
tablespoon
2 mixing bowls
small basin
baking tray
greaseproof paper
(a piece 10 cm or 4 in. square)
oven cloth
electric or gas oven
(300°F – 150°C – mark 2)
washing-up equipment
timer or clock

Ingredients needed:

100 g (4 oz.) desiccated coconut
50 g (2 oz.) sugar
1 egg (Standard or Grade 4)
small knob of lard

Please tell children that they must seek adult help when they see this symbol:

Put on an apron
and roll up your sleeves.

Wash your hands
and scrub your nails
really clean.

These are the ingredients
you will need.
Put them ready on your table.

desiccated coconut
sugar
an egg
lard

This is the equipment you will need. Put it all on your table.

scales
egg cup
teaspoon
fork
tablespoon
2 mixing bowls
small basin
baking tray
greaseproof paper
oven cloth or glove

Set the oven at
300°F (150°C)
if it is electric,
or mark 2
if it is gas.

Turn the oven on.

**Ask a grown-up
to help you.**

Grease the baking tray.
Rub it well,
using the greaseproof paper
and a piece of lard
about the size of a toffee.

Ask a grown-up to show you how.

Weigh 100 grammes
of desiccated coconut.

Put the coconut
into one of the mixing bowls.

Weigh 50 grammes of sugar.

Put the sugar
into the same mixing bowl.

Using the fork,
mix together
the coconut and the sugar.

Break the egg
into the small basin.

Ask a grown-up to show you how.

Using the fork,
whisk the egg well.

Pour the egg
on to the coconut and sugar
in the mixing bowl.

Using the fork,
mix the egg, sugar
and coconut together.

Half fill the other mixing bowl with cold water.

Dip the egg cup
into the cold water
to make it wet.

Fill the egg cup
with the mixture,
pressing it down gently
with the teaspoon.

Turn the egg cup upside down
on to the palm of your hand.

Shake out the coconut pyramid
and then put it
on the baking tray.

Ask a grown-up to show you how.

Keep doing this
until all the mixture
has been used.

Remember to dip the egg cup
in the bowl of water
each time you use it.

Put the coconut pyramids
into the oven.

**Ask a grown-up
to help you.**

Set the timer for 20 minutes
or check the time
on the clock.

After 20 minutes
take the coconut pyramids
from the oven and look at them.

They should feel firm
and be a golden-brown
colour on the top.

**Ask a grown-up
to help you.**

Turn off the oven.

Ask a grown-up to help you.

Wash up
and leave the kitchen
clean and tidy.

Serve the coconut pyramids
by arranging them on a plate.

Eat!

First published 1974 by A. & C. Black Limited
4, 5 & 6 Soho Square, London W1V 6AD
© 1974 A. & C. Black Limited

ISBN 0 7136 1498 6 (net)
     0 7136 1506 0 (non-net)

Printed in England by the Soman-Wherry Press Limited, Norwich